LOVE VEGAN

Mexican Favorites Made Easy

SIDES

OTHER

DESSERT

INTRODUCTION

From Fully Loaded Nachos and Wedges with Vegan Nacho Cheese to Sweet Mexican Rice Milk and Crispy Mexican Churros, this cookbook celebrates the flavours of Mexico and shows you how easy it is to prepare authentic and delicious vegan dishes in your very own kitchen - on even the busiest of weeknights.

Mexican food has become increasingly popular throughout the Western world where you will see Mexican restaurants popping up on your local high street and ready made Mexican meals on the supermarket shelves. Traditional Mexican cuisine is a fusion of the ancient Aztec and Mayan Indians with ingredients and cooking techniques that originated from all over the world including Spanish and Indian influences.

The basic staples of this cuisine come in the form of simple, easy to source, natural ingredients such as corn, pulses and rice - making it very easy to adapt the recipes to the vegan diet.

Our philosophy is to bring an authentic Mexican street food flavour to vegans all over the world and to enable you to enjoy veganised versions of your favorite meals such as Fajitas, Burritos and Chili, along with delicious desserts including Churros and Chili Chocolate Avocado Mousse.

The recipes have been carefully tried, tested and refined to retain an authentic taste and texture, yet uses simple and straight forward ingredients found in your local supermarket. The emphasis is on cooking traditional, authentically flavoured dishes for even the most inexperienced of cooks, making your life simpler and your meal preparation easier.

Whether you are a vegan, vegetarian or meat-eater looking to reduce the amount of animal produce in your diet, the 'Love Vegan' series of cookbooks will inspire you to cook delicious authentically flavoured Mexican vegan dishes on even the busiest of weeknights.

FLAVOURS OF MEXICO

Let's take a look at some of the flavours and staple ingredients from around the country and see how easy it is to adapt them to the vegan diet, while still retaining the taste, texture and delicious Mexican flavour.

Avocado: These creamy and buttery fruits are the perfect compliment to spicy Mexican dishes. They are most commonly used in guacamole but can be used to incorporate a delicious creamy element to any dish.

Pulses: Beans are also known as Frijoles in Mexico, and are a very common ingredient found in a lot of Mexican dishes. The most used pulses in Mexican cuisine are black and pinto beans, which lend their flavour and texture to refried beans - a popular dish made by soaking dried beans, adding spices, and then mashing and frying them.

Cheeses: 'Love Vegan' has some mouth-watering vegan cheese recipes to die for! Whether you are looking for a touch of cheesy flavour to sprinkle on a burrito, or you wish to drizzle some queso on your loaded nachos, this book has some deliciously creamy and flavorsome vegan cheese substitutes that can rival any dairy based version!

Chillies: The most dominant flavour within Mexican food, and most likely what comes to mind when you think of Mexican flavouring. There are many different types that are commonly used including smoked, dried, fresh or picked. Some of the most popular varieties include ancho chillies (mild and sweet), habanero (extremely hot!), jalapeno (the most common) and pasilla (mild to medium heat).

Limes: Lime is widely used throughout Mexican cooking in recipes such as salsa, guacamole and marinades for a burst of zesty fresh flavour.

Tortillas: These soft pancake-like flatbreads are eaten with most Mexican dishes, making the cuisine healthy and dishes lower calorie than others that use bread and pasta.

THE HEALTH BENEFITS OF VEGANISM

'To keep the body in good health is a duty...otherwise we shall not be able to keep our mind strong and clear' - Buddha

There is a growing movement across the Western world where people are becoming more aware of what they are eating and the health and nutritional benefits of food. Healthy eating, along with eliminating or reducing meat intake has become more of a lifestyle decision as opposed to a fad diet.

Veganism is not a fad diet that is only supposed to last for a certain duration. It is a way of life that goes much deeper than just eating plant based food. People choose a vegan diet for many reasons – sometimes it is because they don't want to buy meat from unethical meat farms that treat their animals badly. Other times it is due to a need to simplify their diet to bring their bodies to optimum health.

Vegan foods offer your body high-quality nutrition. The foods are easily digested and are quickly assimilated into your system, thus providing you with an abundance of energy, enough to sustain you for a long period of time.

Beans and legumes are an excellent source of energy, for example, the Black Bean Flautas featured in this book is a lunch option that will keep you feeling full of energy for the entire afternoon. You won't have that lethargic feeling that your body gets when the processed and starchy foods you usually have for lunch have left your body sluggish and tired as all your energy has been taken up trying to digest the heavy carbohydrates in your stomach.

Whether you are a vegan, vegetarian or meat-eater trying to reduce the amount of meat you consume, the 'Love Vegan' cookbook series is here to make your life easier, healthier and most certainly tastier!

MEXICAN PANTRY STAPLES

Mexican dishes are very easy to make as they do not usually feature a lot of ingredients. To make your life easier and to ensure your kitchen is equipt with staple items most commonly used in Mexican cooking it is advisable that you have a well-stocked pantry to avoid a last minute trip to the supermarket after a long day at work.

The list below is a variety of simple and straightforward ingredients that you should keep in your cupboards, ready to whip up a delicious authentic Mexican dish at any time.

- Tinned pulses (black, pinto, butter and kidney beans)
- Tinned tomatoes
- Fresh Garlic
- Fresh Coriander
- Dried Oregano
- Cumin Powder
- Chilis - fresh, dried and powdered
- Vegetable Stock
- Quinoa
- Brown Rice
- Nutritional Yeast (to mimic a 'cheesy' flavour)
- Tofu
- Fresh and Frozen Vegetables (including corn)
- Tortilla wraps (can be frozen)

MEXICAN FAVORITES MADE EASY

Most of us don't want to spend an hour in the kitchen preparing dinner after working all day, however, the 'Love Vegan' Cookbook series proves that you can stay healthy and enjoy quick and easy to cook Mexican cuisine on even the busiest of weeknights. The best part is that most recipes will take less than half an hour to prepare.

The type of Mexican cuisine you would find in restaurants relies heavily on meat, cheese and dishes that are high in carbs. Finding vegan cheese can be a challenge and is likely to have chemicals and preservatives in it, but now you can make your own within this recipe book. It is easy and you can flavour it with whatever spice you want.

Mexican food need not be complicated to make. Our featured recipes contain basic, straightforward, wholesome and natural ingredients that you can easily find in your local supermarket or farmer's market. The aim of this book and the 'Love Vegan' series is to make eating vegan food a pleasure as well as filling your body with nourishing food that is quick to prepare.

There is no better way to mark special occasions than with tasty homemade food. From birthdays, Thanksgiving or Christmas to a lazy family Sunday BBQ - we have the perfect vegan option for every occasion. Put in your tender loving flair and you will create a mouthwatering array of recipes that will leave you feeling like a professional chef.

SUMMARY

We love Mexican food because its dishes are spicy, colorful, and full of flavor.

This cookbook is focused on basic, natural and wholesome ingredients, and when cooked in the right way and perfectly flavoured you can create beautiful, authentic and mouth-watering vegan dishes, regardless of your cooking ability.

Whether you are a long term follower of the vegan lifestyle, a beginner in need of an easy way to get started or a meat-eater looking to incorporate a meat-free Monday into the week, this book will give you some deliciously authentic recipes for any occasion.

So get ready for some exciting and easy to cook vegan meals that will open up a whole new world for you.

MAINS

MEXICAN WEDGES WITH VEGAN NACHO CHEESE SAUCE

Crisp and fluffy Mexican spiced wedges with creamy melted nacho cheese, and best of all this dish is 100% vegan! The cheese sauce is so versatile you can use it with other recipes.

Preparation Time: **Total Time:**   Makes 4 servings
15 minutes   50 minutes

INGREDIENTS

FOR THE POTATO WEDGES:

3 large white potatoes, cut into wedges (you can decide if you prefer the skin on or off)
2 tsp olive oil
2 tsp ground cumin
1 tsp ground coriander
1 tsp garlic powder
1 ½ tsp paprika
½ - 1 tsp cayenne pepper (depends on how spicy you want them to be)
1 tsp dried oregano
½ tsp coarse salt
½ tsp freshly ground black pepper
2 tbsp fresh coriander. roughly chopped

FOR THE NACHO CHEESE SAUCE:

2 medium potatoes, scrubbed and chopped
3 large carrots, scrubbed, peeled and chopped
½ cup nutritional yeast
⅓ cup olive oil (use extra virgin if possible)
⅓ cup water
1 tbsp freshly squeezed lemon juice
1½ tsp coarse salt
1-2 jalapenos, finely chopped (optional)

DIRECTIONS

To make the Potato Wedges:

Preheat the oven to 180°C. Grease a baking tray with a little olive oil.

Place the potato wedges in large mixing bowl and add the oil, cumin, garlic, coriander, paprika, cayenne, dried oregano and seasoning. Mix well until fully combined and each potato wedge is coated with the flavouring.

Transfer wedges to the greased baking tray and move them around so that they are in a single layer. This will enable them to get really crispy. If you find there are too many to fit on your baking tray you may need to use two.

Bake the wedges for 35-40 minutes, flipping them over once halfway through cooking.

While the wedges are baking you can prepare the Cheese Sauce.

For the Nacho Cheese Sauce:

Place potatoes and carrots in a steamer and steam until soft and tender. If you do not have a steamer you can boil the vegetables using the following method: Place potatoes, carrots and ½ tsp salt in a saucepan and fill with just enough water to cover. Bring to a boil and allow to cook for 5-7 minutes until tender when pierced with a fork.

Once the vegetables have cooked add to a food processor and blend along with nutritional yeast, olive oil, water, lemon juice and salt until smooth and creamy.

Remove from blender and stir in chopped jalapenos.

Remove wedges from the oven and transfer to a serving plate. Garnish with chopped coriander and serve with the nacho cheese. You can either drizzle the cheese on top or serve it on the side as a dip.

FULLY LOADED NACHOS

There are three different recipes that you will need to prepare beforehand - cheese sauce, salsa and chili, but believe us when we say it will be worth your while! You can serve this dish without any one of these elements if you wish to reduce the preparation time, however, it is highly recommended to include all three!

Preparation Time:	Total Time:	Makes 2-3 as a
10 minutes	15 minutes (+ additional time to make the cheese sauce, salsa and chili)	main course or 6-8 as an appetiser

INGREDIENTS

1 large bag tortilla chips
2 cup Nacho Cheese Sauce
1 cup Mexican Salsa
2 cups Quinoa Chili
1 can black beans
1 large tomato, chopped
¾ cup corn

4-5 spring onions chopped
1 avocado, peeled, pitted and chopped
2-3 jalapenos, finely chopped
¼ cup fresh coriander, roughly chopped
½ cup sliced black olives

DIRECTIONS

Layer ⅓ of chips at the bottom then dollop with ⅓ chili and ⅓ salsa. Drizzle with ⅓ of cheese sauce, then sprinkle with half of black beans.

Layer with another ⅓ of chips and dollop with ⅓ chili and ⅓ salsa. Drizzle with ⅓ of cheese sauce, then sprinkle with remaining half of black beans.

Layer with remaining ⅓ of chips and dollop with ⅓ chili and ⅓ salsa. Drizzle with 1/3 of cheese sauce.

Top with the salsa, tomatoes, corn, spring onions, olives, jalapeños, avocado, and coriander. Serve immediately.

The nachos will keep in an airtight container in the fridge and will last 3-5 days.

BLACK BEAN FLAUTAS

A flauta is a traditional Mexican dish consisting of a rolled up tortilla, which has been stuffed with a choice of filling and then fried to create a golden crispy exterior. These authentically flavoured flautas are perfect as a main dish with rice or as an appetiser.

Preparation Time: 15 minutes (+ 15 minutes for the sauce to marinate)

Total Time: 30 minutes

Makes 16 flautas / Serves 3-4

INGREDIENTS

½ cup red onion, finely chopped
¼ cup fresh coriander leaves, chopped
1 large lime, freshly juiced
1 garlic clove, peeled and finely chopped
1 large lime, cut into wedges
2 cups refried beans

16 white corn tortillas, warmed
Vegetable or canola oil for frying
¼ head chopped lettuce
1 tomato, chopped

Toothpicks to hold flautas together while cooking

DIRECTIONS

In a small bowl combine red onion, coriander, lime and garlic and set aside for 10-15 minutes to marinate. Stir occasionally.

In a small bowl, combine the red onion, chopped cilantro, and lime juice. Set aside to marinate, stirring occasionally.

Heat ¼ inch of oil in a frying pan over medium heat.

Lay warmed tortilla out on a clean surface or chopping board and spread 1 heaped tablespoon of refried beans and ½ tablespoon of coriander-lime mixture evenly over one side of the tortilla. Starting from the filling side, tightly roll each tortilla then secure it with a toothpick so it doesn't come undone while cooking. It is advised to roll around 3-4 at a time, fry these, and roll 4 more while each batch is cooking.

Fry the batch of flautas, seam side down for 4-5 minutes, gently flipping over once halfway through frying using a pair of tongs. Once they are golden brown and crisp on all sides remove the flautas using the tongs and transfer to a paper towel lined plate.

Continue with remaining tortilla wraps, and remove the toothpick once they have cooled down a little and are ready to serve.

Serve immediately while hot a crispy with lettuce, tomato and a dipping sauce of your choice. Sour Cream or Chimichurri works well.

QUINOA CHILI

This vegan, protein-packed chili is the perfect bowl of comfort food that is loaded with fresh pulses and quinoa, and packed full of spicy Mexican flavour.

Preparation Time: **Total Time:** Makes 6 servings
10 minutes 40 minutes

INGREDIENTS

¾ cups uncooked quinoa + 1 ½ cups water

1 tbsp olive oil

1 large onion, finely chopped

4 garlic cloves, minced

1-2 fresh chilies, finely chopped

2 (420g) cans chopped tomatoes

1 (420g) can tomato sauce

1 ½ cups vegetable stock

1 tbsp chili powder

1 tbsp cayenne pepper

1 tbsp cumin

1 tbsp paprika

1 tsp dried oregano

1 level tsp ground coriander

1 tsp white sugar

1 tsp coarse salt

¾ tsp freshly ground pepper

2 (420g) can kidney beans, drained and rinsed

1 (15 oz) can black or pinto beans, drained and rinsed

1 ½ cups corn, fresh or frozen

½ cup coriander, chopped

Juice of 1 lime, freshly squeezed

DIRECTIONS

In a large saucepan heat olive oil, then add chopped onions and saute for 3-4 minutes until soft. Add garlic and fresh chili and cook for a further minute.

Add the cumin powder, chili, cayenne, paprika and oregano and stir for 30 seconds until fragrant.

Pour in the 2 cans of chopped tomatoes, tomato sauce, vegetable stock, dry quinoa. Bring to a boil then reduce to a low simmer. Cover and simmer over low heat for 20 minutes.

Uncover, add beans, corn, coriander, lime juice and seasoning, and cook uncovered for 10 minutes until the sauce has reduced and thickened.

SPICY SWEET POTATO BURGERS WITH AVOCADO

These are such versatile burgers that can be eaten inside a bun or alone for a lower carb meal. The beans help the burger hold together to create a firm, flavorful and filling patty.

Preparation Time:	**Total Time:**	Makes 8 patties /
10 minutes	1 hour and 10 minutes (including cooking time for sweet potato)	Serves 4 people

INGREDIENTS

1 large sweet potato, peeled
450g can of white beans, drained and rinsed
½ cup white onion, chopped
2-3 tbsp tahini
1 tsp apple cider vinegar
1 tsp garlic powder
1 ½ tsp cajun spice (or cayenne pepper for spicier burgers)
½ tsp freshly ground black pepper

½ tsp coarse salt
⅓ cup all-purpose flour (you can also use coconut or almond flour)
8 Burger buns (optional)

FOR THE TOPPINGS:

1 large avocado, peeled, pitted and sliced
1 large tomato, sliced
¼ head lettuce, chopped

DIRECTIONS

Preheat the oven to 200°C and grease a baking tray lightly with oil. Bake the sweet potato for around 45 minutes, or until the inside of soft and tender. If you do not have time you could cheat and cook it in the microwave. To do this leave the potato unpeeled and pierce the skin 5-6 times, place on a microwaveable plate, cover and microwave for 8-10 minutes, rotating halfway through.

Around 10 minutes before the potato is due to come out of the oven (or while it is in the microwave), place the drained and rinsed beans in a saucepan of boiling hot water and cook on high for 8-10 minutes in order to soften them.

In a large bowl combine potato and beans and use a potato masher or large fork to mash together. Add the onions, tahini, vinegar, garlic powder, cajun spice, salt, pepper and flour and continue to mash until the mixture has thickened and all ingredients are well combined.

Preheat oven to 200°C. Grease a baking tray with some oil.

Equally divide potato mixture into 8 patties, shaping and flattening them into a round burger shape then place on the greased baking tray. Bake for 10-15 minutes, carefully turning each burger half way through with a spatula.

A few minutes before the burgers are due to come out of the oven lightly toast the buns.

Serve burgers straight from the oven while warm crisp and golden. Garnish with avocado, tomato and lettuce.

They will store for 1-2 days in the fridge or 4 weeks in the freezer.

ROASTED SWEET POTATO & BEAN QUESADILLAS

This easy and delicious meatless meal combines mashed sweet potatoes with hearty and filling refried beans for a satisfying and crowd-pleasing meal. You could also serve this with a side of Vegan Sour Cream to add a creamy element.

Preparation Time:	Total Time:	Serves 2 as a
10 minutes	55 minutes (including cooking time for sweet potato)	main or 4 as a side dish

INGREDIENTS

2 medium sweet potatoes, peeled and sliced

4 tbsp olive oil, divided

2 tsp cumin powder

2 tsp paprika powder

½ tsp coarse salt

4 white tortillas

¼ tsp freshly ground black pepper

2 cups refried beans

2 tbsp jalapenos, finely chopped

1 avocado, peeled, pitted and chopped

DIRECTIONS

Preheat the oven to 210°C.

In a small bowl combine 2 tablespoons of oil, cumin, paprika, salt and pepper. Place the sweet potatoes in a baking dish and pour the oil spice mixture over, coating all sides of the potato.

Bake in the oven for 40 minutes or until the potatoes are cooked throughout and slightly caramelised on the edges.

Heat a large frying pan with oil over medium heat. Place the tortilla on the plate and spread with ¼ of the sweet potato mix, ¼ of the refried beans and a few chunks of avocado over half of the tortilla wrap, then fold it over. Carefully transfer it to the frying pan using either a spatula or by very carefully sliding the tortilla from the plate onto the pan. Press down using the spatula and cook for 2-3 minutes on each side.

Remove from heat and transfer to a serving plate.

Repeat with remaining wraps and filling and serve while hot and crispy.

AVOCADO ENCHILADAS

These mouthwatering vegan black bean & avocado enchiladas are stuffed with fresh ingredients and smothered in a homemade enchilada sauce for an authentic Mexican experience, any night of the week.

Preparation Time: 15 minutes

Total Time: 45 minutes

Makes 6 enchiladas

INGREDIENTS

2 tbsp olive or vegetable oil
2 medium garlic cloves, finely chopped
1 white onion, sliced
1 red bell pepper, sliced
1 (420g) can black beans, drained and rinsed
1 (420g) can chickpeas, drained and rinsed
2 large avocados, peeled, pitted and chopped
⅓ cup nutritional yeast
3 medium tomatoes, chopped
2 tsp cumin powder
1 tsp paprika
½ tsp cayenne pepper
½ tsp salt
¼ tsp pepper
6 large tortillas

FOR THE ENCHILADA SAUCE:

2 tbsp olive or vegetable oil
3 cups vegetable stock
¼ cup tomato puree
¼ cup all-purpose flour
2 tbsp olive oil
2 tsp cumin powder
½ tsp chili powder
¼ tsp garlic powder
¼ tsp onion powder
½ tsp dried oregano
½ tsp coarse salt
½ tsp freshly ground black pepper

DIRECTIONS

Heat a large frying pan with oil over medium heat. Once hot add onions and peppers and saute for 4-5 minutes until soft. Add garlic and fry for 1-2 minutes.

Reduce heat to low and add cumin, paprika and cayenne, stirring constantly for 30 seconds until the spices are fragrant.

Add the chopped tomatoes, avocado, nutritional yeast, black band and chickpeas and mix well. Heat for 5-6 minutes then remove from heat and set aside.

Next prepare the enchilada sauce. In a small bowl combine flour, cumin, chili, garlic, onion and oregano.

Heat a frying pan with oil over medium heat. Once hot add the tomato paste and fry, moving it around frequently for 30 seconds. Slowly add the flour and spice mixture and mix well to combine. Allow to cook for 30 seconds to 1 minutes using a whisk to stir constantly.

Pour in the vegetable stock and bring mixture to a boil, then reduce heat and simmer for 8-10 minutes until the sauce has thickened and reduced.

Preheat the oven to 175°C and grease a 9x13 inch oven dish with a little oil.

Place tortilla wraps on a clean surface and evenly distribute bean mixture between the 6 wraps, rolling each one tightly and tuck in the ends then transfer to the greased oven dish.

Pour over the enchilada sauce, covering each wrap and bake for 25 minutes.

Serve immediately while hot.

MEXICAN QUINOA

Easy to make, versatile and extremely flavorsome, this Mexican spiced quinoa is a fail-proof recipe which will compliment most main meals perfectly. Try serving it with a salad or refried beans.

Preparation Time: **Total Time:**   Makes 4 servings
10 minutes   35 minutes

INGREDIENTS

1 tbsp olive oil
2 cloves garlic, finely chopped
1 jalapeno, finely chopped
1 cup uncooked quinoa
1 cup vegetable stock
1 (420g) can kidney beans, drained and rinsed
1 (420g) can chopped tomatoes
1 cup corn kernels, fresh or frozen
1 tsp chili powder

1 tsp cumin powder
1 tsp paprika
½ tsp coarse salt
½ tsp freshly ground black pepper
1 avocado, peeled pitted and diced
1 lime, freshly juiced
2 tbsp fresh coriander leaves, chopped

DIRECTIONS

Heat olive oil in a large saucepan or pot over medium heat. Once hot add the garlic and jalapenos and cook, stirring frequently, for 1 minute. Add chili powder, cumin and paprika and stir frequently for 30 seconds.

Stir in quinoa, vegetable stock, beans, chopped tomato, corn and seasoning and bring to a boil.

Reduce heat to low, cover the pot, and simmer for 20 minutes.

Remove from heat, uncover and stir in avocado, lime juice and chopped coriander,

Transfer to a serving bowl and serve immediately.

TOFU FAJITAS

The word "Fajita" derives from the Spanish word "Faja," meaning strip. In this recipe you'll use strips of beautifully flavoured tofu and bake them in a sticky Mexican glaze before wrapping them in tortillas along with fresh veggies.

Preparation Time: 10 minutes (+ 10 minutes to marinade the tofu)

Total Time: 40 minutes

Makes 4 servings

INGREDIENTS

450g extra-firm tofu, sliced into long thin strips
½ cup light soy sauce
4 tbsp vegetable oil, divided
1 tbsp brown sugar or maple syrup
2 tbsp nutritional yeast (optional)
½ -1 tsp cayenne pepper
1 tsp cumin powder

1 tsp dried oregano
2 tbsp oil
1 small carrot, thinly sliced
1 red bell pepper, thinly sliced,
1 portobello mushroom, thinly sliced
2 tbsp fresh coriander, roughly chopped
4 large tortilla wraps

DIRECTIONS

In a medium bowl combine soy sauce, maple syrup or sugar, nutritional yeast, cayenne pepper, cumin, oregano and 2 tbsp oil. Add the tofu, coating well, and leave to marinade for a minimum of 10 minutes.

Preheat the oven to 170°C. Line a baking tray with baking paper.

Place the tofu on the baking tray in a single layer and pour the sauce over.

Bake for 30 minutes, turning twice. Remove from the oven and set aside.

Heat a frying pan over medium-high heat with 2 tbsp oil and saute vegetables for 5 minutes. Add tofu and coriander and cook for a further minute.

Place the tortillas in a warm oven or the microwave for 30 seconds-1 minute until soft and warm.

Place ¼ filling in a tortilla and wrap tightly. Continue with remaining filling and wraps. Serve immediately while hot.

CHILI CON VEGGIE

This brilliant alternative to the classic chilli con carne is rich, hearty and meat-free. It's packed full of pulses, high in fibre and has a welcoming kick of chili!

Preparation Time: **Total Time:**   Makes 4 servings
10 minutes   1 hour and 10 minutes

INGREDIENTS

1 tbsp olive oil
1 large onion, finely chopped
2 large garlic cloves, finely chopped
1 fresh red chilli
1 tbsp cumin powder
1 tbsp ground coriander
1 tbsp paprika
½ - 1 tsp cayenne powder (depending on spice preference)
1 tbsp dried oregano
½ tbsp dried parsley
1 medium carrot, finely chopped

1 heaped tbsp tomato purée
250g dried red lentils
1 can (420g) red kidney beans, drained and rinsed
1 can (420g) pinto or navy beans, drained or rinsed
1 can (420g) chopped tomatoes
600ml vegetable stock
1 tsp coarse salt
¾ tsp freshly ground black pepper
2 tbsp fresh coriander, roughly chopped

DIRECTIONS

Heat olive oil in a large pot over medium heat. Once hot add onions and saute for 3-4 minutes then add garlic, cumin, paprika, oregano, parsley and cayenne and fry for a further minute.

Add the carrot, mixing well and pour in the two cans of beans. Crush a few of the beans using a fork or a wooden spoon. This will give the chili a thicker and creamier texture.

Add the tomato puree and stir constantly for 30 seconds then add the lentils and pour in the chopped tomato and stock. Bring to a boil then reduce to a low simmer and cook for 1 hour, stirring occasionally.

Remove from heat, season, then stir in chopped coriander and serve over rice or inside a tortilla wrap.

SPICY BLACK BEAN SOUP

This spicy soup uses basic store cupboard ingredients and is cooked from scratch. It features sautéed onions, hearty black beans and creamy avocado - all simmered in a delicious Mexican spiced broth.

Preparation Time: **Total Time:**   Makes 4 servings
10 minutes   20 mins

INGREDIENTS

2 tbsp olive oil
1 small onion, chopped
2 garlic cloves, finely chopped
1 large bell pepper, chopped
1 can of black beans, rinsed and drained
500ml vegetable stock
½ cup fresh coriander, roughly chopped

1 tbsp ground cumin
1 tbsp paprika
1 ½ tsp oregano
½ tsp cayenne pepper
½ - 1 tsp dried chili flakes (depending on spice)
1 ½ tbsp balsamic vinegar
1 avocado, peeled, pitted and chopped

DIRECTIONS

Heat olive oil in a large pot over medium heat. Once hot add onions and saute for 3-4 minutes then add garlic, cumin, paprika, oregano, dried chili and cayenne and fry for a further minute.

Add the pepper, mixing well and pour in the can of black beans. Crush a few of the beans using a fork or a wooden spoon. This will give the soup a thicker and creamier texture.

Pour in the vegetable stock and bring mixture to a boil.

Reduce to a simmer then add balsamic vinegar and chopped coriander. Allow to simmer on low for 10 minutes for the flavours to marry.

Add the avocado then serve immediately while hot.

QUINOA STUFFED PEPPERS

Serve these vibrant stuffed peppers on any occasion, from a busy weeknight to guests at a dinner party - and you can then keep the leftovers for lunch the following day! Not only are they quick to make but they are also stuffed with fresh veggies.

Preparation Time: 10 minutes

Total Time: 20 minutes

Makes 4-6 servings

INGREDIENTS

½ cup quinoa, uncooked
1 cups vegetable stock
¼ can (approx 100g) black beans, rinsed and drained
½ medium carrot, grated
1 celery stalks, finely chopped
¼ medium onion, finely diced
2 cloves garlic, minced
¼ cup peas, fresh or frozen

¼ cup corn, fresh or frozen
½ tsp onion powder
½ tsp garlic powder
½ tsp coarse salt
½ tsp freshly ground pepper
½ tsp cayenne pepper
½ tsp cumin powder
½ cup tomato sauce
4 bell peppers, any color

DIRECTIONS

Preheat the oven to 170°C. Line a small ovenproof dish (5x10-inch) with baking paper and set aside.

Bring 2 cups of vegetable stock to a boil then add quinoa. Stir, the cover and allow to cook for around 15 minutes then drain any excess water and set aside.

In a large saucepan mix beans, grated carrot, celery, onions, garlic, peas, corn and all spices together and heat for around 7 minutes over medium-low heat.

Add cooked quinoa and tomato sauce, mixing well, and heat for a further 5 minutes.

While the vegetable mixture is cooked you can prepare the peppers.

Cut the top off each bell pepper and place in the ovenproof dish, Stuff each pepper with the quinoa mixture and transfer to the oven.

Bake for 30-35 minutes until the pepper has softened and the top has browned.

WHITE BEAN & AVOCADO BURRITOS

This easy, filling and delicious dish is sure to become one of your go-to weeknight meals. They are baked in the oven, making this tasty Mexican meal super healthy.

Preparation Time: 25 minutes

Total Time: 50 minutes

Makes 4 servings

INGREDIENTS

FOR THE RICE:

1 cups brown rice
1 cup vegetable stock
1 cup water

FOR THE FILLING:

½ cup vegetable stock
3 cloves garlic, finely chopped
1 medium onions, chopped
1 ½ tsp cumin powder
3 cups mushrooms, chopped (any variety)
2 bell peppers, sliced (any colour)
1 jalapeno peppers, finely chopped
1 tbsp fresh coriander, chopped
1 ½ cups white beans (Butter beans, Cannellini beans etc)

¼ cup tomato sauce
2 tbsp cup nutritional yeast (optional but recommended)
½ tsp coarse salt
½ tsp freshly ground black pepper
¾ cup corn, fresh or frozen

FOR THE TOMATO SAUCE:

2 cups plain tomato sauce
1½ tsp garlic powder
1 ½ tsp onion powder
1 tbsp granulated sugar
2 tbsp fresh coriander, chopped
1 tsp cumin

FOR THE BURRITOS:

2 large avocados, peeled pitted and chopped
8 large tortilla wraps

DIRECTIONS

Preheat the oven to 180°C. Grease one or two large casserole dish (around 9x13).

To Make the Rice:

Pour water and vegetable stock into a saucepan and bring to a boil. Add rice, cover and simmer for 15-17 minutes until cooked. Set aside.

To Make the Burrito Filling:

Heat 1 tbsp vegetable oil in a large pot over medium-high heat and saute the onions for 3-4 minutes until soft. Add the garlic and cumin and cook for a further minute.

Pour in a splash of the vegetable broth and add the mushrooms, peppers and jalapenos, frying for 3-4 minutes until the vegetables have softened.

Pour in the remaining vegetable stock along with the white beans, coriander, tomato sauce, nutritional yeast and seasoning. Heat the mixture for 4-5 minutes.

Remove from heat and very carefully transfer ⅓ of the burrito filling into a blender or food processor and blend until a type of puree forms. Add it back into the pot of beans and stir in corn. Set aside.

To Make the Tomato Sauce:

In a medium bowl mix together garlic powder, onion powder, sugar, coriander and cumin.

To Assemble the Burritos:

Lay the tortilla wrap on a clean surface such as a chopping board or large plate.

Fill with just under ½ cup of burrito filling, ¼ cup rice and a small handful of avocado. Wrap tightly and tuck in the ends.

Continue with remaining filling and wraps. Place each burrito seam side down and bake in the oven for 25 minutes.

There may be some leftover rice and burrito filling which will keep well for up for 4 days in an airtight container in the fridge.

FAJITA PASTA

This recipe is super easy - you simply throw all of the ingredients into a big pot and leave it to allow the flavours to marry together while the pasta is cooking. Clean up is easy too as you need just one pot to cook the entire meal!

Preparation Time: **Total Time:**   Makes 4-6 servings
10 minutes   20 minutes

INGREDIENTS

450g linguine
2 (420g) can chopped tomatoes
1 cup vegetable stock
2 tbsp chili sauce (e.g. Sriracha)
1 large red onion, thinly sliced
8 cloves garlic, finely chopped
1 large red bell pepper, thinly sliced
1 yellow pepper, thinly sliced
1 tsp dried chili flakes
½ tbsp coarse salt

1 tsp cumin
1 tsp paprika
¾ tsp chili powder
1 tsp dried oregano
2 tbsp coriander, plus extra for garnish
3 tbsp olive oil
½ tsp freshly ground pepper
2 cups water
1 lime, cut into wedges

DIRECTIONS

In a large pot add dry linguine, tomatoes, vegetable stock, chili sauce, onion, garlic, peppers, dried chili flakes, cumin, paprika, chili powder, coriander, oil, pepper and water.

Bring mixture to a boil and cook for 10-12 minutes until the sauce has thickened and reduced, stirring frequently.

Serve immediately and garnish with lime wedges and chopped coriander.

SIDES

MEXICAN GAZPACHO

This refreshing chilled soup is perfect for a warm summers evening or served at a BBQ. It packs a healthy punch, filled with ingredients like tomato, peppers and cucumber.

Preparation Time: **Total Time:**   Makes 4 servings
5 minutes   10 minutes

INGREDIENTS

1 ¼ cups cucumber, chopped and peeled, divided
½ cup red or green bell pepper, chopped
2 tbsp red onion, finely chopped
1 tbsp jalapeño pepper, finely chopped
1 tbsp white vinegar
½ tsp sugar

¼ tsp coarse salt
½ tsp dried oregano
¼ to ½ tsp tabasco or other hot sauce
1 garlic clove, chopped
1 (420g) can chopped tomatoes
¾ cup vegetable stock
Handful of fresh basil leaves, roughly chopped

DIRECTIONS

Place 1 cup cucumber, pepper, red onion, jalapeño pepper, white vinegar, sugar, salt, dried oregano, tabasco sauce and garlic in a food processor and pulse until well combined and broken down but not completely smooth. If you prefer your gazpacho completely smooth feel free to blend for longer.

Remove from food processor and pour into a large bowl. Stir in water, chopped tomatoes and fresh basil leaves. Cover with cling film and chill in the fridge for a minimum of 2 hours, preferably overnight.

When you are ready to serve, divide the soup into 4 bowls and top each bowl with 1 tablespoon of chopped cucumber.

CORIANDER LIME RICE

A delicious dish that can be eaten alone or as the perfect accompaniment for Mexican main dishes. The fresh lime and coriander really brings this meal to life and transforms plain rice into something very special.

Preparation Time: **Total Time:**   Makes 4 servings
5 minutes   20 minutes

INGREDIENTS

1 cup uncooked dry rice (long grain is the best to use)
2 cups water + ½ tsp salt

1 large lime, juiced and zested
½ cup fresh coriander, chopped
1 tsp coarse salt

DIRECTIONS

Place 2 cups water and salt in a saucepan and bring to a boil. Stir in rice and cover. Reduce the heat to low and simmer for 15-17 minutes without removing the lid.

Add lime juice, zest, coriander and salt and mix well to combine.

Transfer to a serving plate and serve immediately while hot.

CLASSIC GUACAMOLE

A classic dish that requires no introduction. This tried and tested recipe is simple, quick and incredibly tasty. You can keep it smooth or chunky, and if you don't plan to serve it immediately just leave the avocado pit in the guacamole bowl to prevent any browning.

Preparation Time: **Total Time:** Makes 4-6 servings
5 minutes 5 minutes

INGREDIENTS

4 ripe avocados, peeled, pitted and chopped (save the stone if not serving immediately)
2 tbsp lime juice, freshly squeezed
1 medium ripe tomato, seeded and chopped
1 jalapeno, finely chopped

1 garlic clove, finely chopped
½ small red onion, finely chopped
½ cup fresh cilantro leaves, chopped
½ tsp coarse salt
¼ tsp freshly ground black pepper

DIRECTIONS

Lightly mash the avocado in a medium bowl then add remaining ingredients, mixing well but gently to avoid crushing the avocado too much. You want to keep it chunky so that it retains a nice texture.

If you're not serving straight away, sit a stone in the guacamole (this helps to stop it going brown), cover with cling film and chill until needed.

REFRIED BEANS

'Frijoles Refritos' is a traditional staple dish in Mexico and consists of cooked beans that have been authentically spiced and then mashed, transforming a rather boring side dish to a flavor-packed feature!

Preparation Time:
10 minutes (+ 1 ½ - 2 hours to cook the beans*)

Total Time:
20 minutes

Makes 4-6 servings

*You can use 2 (420g) cans tinned beans to save time

INGREDIENTS

1 cup (225g) dried pinto or black beans

2 sprigs fresh oregano or 1 tsp dried oregano

1 medium white onion, finely chop half and leave the other half whole

½ tsp cumin powder

½ - 1 tsp chili powder

2 medium garlic cloves, unpeeled

¾ tsp coarse salt

6 tbsp vegetable oil

DIRECTIONS

Place the dry beans into a large pot and pour in enough water to cover the beans by around 2 inches. Add the oregano, whole half onion and garlic cloves and bring mixture to a boil. Reduce to a simmer and cook for 1 ½ - 2 hours until the beans are tender.

Drain the beans and set aside 3 cups (save any remaining beans for use in another dish), reserve the liquid the bean cooked in and discard the oregano sprig, onion and garlic.

Heat a large frying pan with vegetable oil and once hot add the chopped onion, cooking over medium heat for 5-6 minutes until soft. Add the cumin and chili powder and stir constantly or 30 seconds.

Pour in the beans and mix well, cooking over low heat for 2 minutes, then add 1 cup of the liquid the beans cooked in. Using a potato masher or the back of a wooden spoon mash the beans until a chunky 'puree' has formed. You can mash according to your preference.

Season with salt and pepper then cook the refried beans for 2-3 minutes until desired consistency is reached. If they appear to be drying out simply add more bean-liquid, one tablespoon at a time.

CREAMY MEXICAN KALE & SPINACH SALAD

This salad is a slightly altered version of a traditional Mexican street salad which combines super healthy kale and spinach with beans and corn, all tossed in a sensationally flavorsome creamy avocado dressing.

Preparation Time: 5 minutes

Total Time: 5 minutes

Makes 6 servings

INGREDIENTS

FOR THE SALAD:

2 packed cups kale, washed, stalks removed & roughly chopped

2 packed cups spinach, washed, stems removed & roughly chopped

1 (420g) can kidney beans, drained and rinsed

1 cup corn, fresh or frozen

2 bell peppers (any colour), finely chopped

1 ½ large avocado, peeled, pitted and finely chopped

1 large tomato, finely chopped

½ small red onion, finely chopped

½ cup coriander, finely chopped

1 tbsp jalapeño peppers, seeded & minced

FOR THE DRESSING:

½ large avocado

½ cup warm water

½ lime, freshly squeezed

1 tsp cumin

¾ tsp salt

½ tsp freshly ground black pepper

DIRECTIONS

Combine all salad ingredients in a large bowl. Set aside.

Add all dressing ingredients to a food processor or blender and pulse until smooth.

If you plan to consume the salad in one day then pour the dressing over the salad, mixing well. However, if you think you will have leftovers it is better to add dressing when you need as it will make the salad slightly soggy and brown a little. To keep, refrigerate separately for 24 hours.

7 LAYER MEXICAN DIP

This recipe combines various other side dishes and layers them all together to create a delicious, exciting and surprisingly healthy dip. If each element is readily available the recipe takes no time, however, if you need to prepare each layer it will take longer- but will certainly be worth it!

Preparation Time: **Total Time:** Makes 8-10 servings
10 mins 10 mins (Assembly
time only)

INGREDIENTS

2 cups refried beans, store bought or homemade

¾ cup Vegan Mexican 'Queso'

1 cup guacamole, store-bought or homemade

1 cup salsa, store bought or homemade

½ bell pepper, chopped

1 handful black olives, roughly chopped

1 handful fresh cilantro, chopped

Large bag of tortilla chips, for serving

DIRECTIONS

To Assemble the Dip:

Take a large bowl and spread an even layer of the refried beans on the bottom. Next spread the Queso Cheese, then guacamole. Top with salsa, a layer of red peppers and finally sprinkle olives and coriander on top.

Serve immediately or cover tightly with cling film and store in the fridge for 1 day.

VEGAN ELOTE (MEXICAN STREET CORN)

This popular Mexican street food is easy to replicate at home for an authentic flavour of South America. The corn is slathered in a delicious creamy chili and lime sauce and then grilled to perfection.

Preparation Time:
5 minutes (+ 1-hour minimum for cashew nuts to soak)

Total Time:
20 minutes

Makes 4 servings

INGREDIENTS

4 corn on the cobs, husk and string fully removed
1 cup raw cashew nuts
½ cup water
½ tbsp apple cider vinegar
½ tsp dried chili flakes
½ tsp cayenne powder
½ tsp cumin powder
½ tsp paprika

½ tsp turmeric powder
1 garlic clove, peeled and finely chopped
Juice of one lime, freshly squeezed
2 tbsp fresh coriander, roughly chopped
Olive oil, for greasing baking tray

DIRECTIONS

Place cashew nuts in a small bowl and top with water, vinegar, lime juice, chili flakes, cayenne, cumin, paprika, turmeric and garlic. Leave for at least 1-hour, or up to 4.

Pour cashew nuts and liquid into a blender and pulse until fully combined.

Preheat the grill to high heat and line a baking tray with foil. Drizzle a little olive oil on the baking tray.

Bring a saucepan of water to a rolling boil and carefully drop in corn, boiling for 3 minutes.

Remove and discard water. Pat corn dry with a kitchen towel to remove as much water as possible.

Transfer corn to the baking tray and coat evenly with the cashew mixture.

Grill corn for 10-15 minutes, turning once or twice.

Remove from grill and garnish with coriander.

OTHER

BOLILLOS (MEXICAN BREAD ROLLS)

These fluffy, warm and crisp Mexican rolls are most commonly eaten by cutting one end off, scooping out the insides and stuffing it with a filling of your choice such as refried beans, salsa or chili.

Preparation Time:	Total Time:	Makes 12 rolls
40 minutes	2 hours 50 minutes (including time for the dough to rise)	

INGREDIENTS

2 ¼ tsp or 1 package active dry yeast

2 cups warm water (between 105°F and 115°F)

1 tsp sugar

4 – 4 ½ cups bread flour

1 tsp coarse salt

1 tsp vegetable shortening

Good quality olive oil for greasing

DIRECTIONS

Place the yeast and sugar in a small mixing bowl and stir in the water. Leave for 5 minutes for the mixture to froth and bubble. If it does not then your yeast is inactive and you will need to start again.

Break the shortening into small pieces and add to the yeast mixture, along with salt and 3 cups of flour. Mix on low using a stand mixer fitted with a dough attachment or using your hands. If the dough appears a little too sticky add a tablespoon of flour at a time in order for it to come together.

Knead by hand or using your stand mixer on low for around 10 minutes. The dough needs to be soft, smooth, and elastic. It should ping back when a finger is pressed into it.

Lightly grease a large bowl with a little olive oil and place the dough inside, turning it over to coat all sides. Cover with a damp kitchen towel and leave undisturbed in a warm place for 1 - 1 ½ hours or until the dough has doubled in size.

Grease a baking sheet with a little olive oil and set aside.

Dump the dough onto a clean lightly floured surface and knead for 1-2 minutes, then roll into a log and using a knife divide into 12 even pieces. Roll each piece between your palms and make an oval shape, tapering the ends a little.

Transfer each roll onto the greased baking tray, ensuring both sides are coated with oil. Repeat with remaining dough then place a kitchen towel on top and set aside for 40 minutes in a warm place for them to rise again.

After 40 minutes, preheat the oven to 190°C. The rolls should have doubled in size again.

Score each roll a few times using a sharp knife, starting at the tapered side and working your way down in horizontal swipes.

Gently brush each roll with a little more olive oil then bake in the preheated oven for 27-30 minutes until golden brown.

Remove from the oven and allow to cool for a few minutes on a wire rack.

Serve immediately while warm and crusty or leave to cool for later.

They will keep at room temperature in an airtight container for up to 3 days, and you can reheat them in the oven at 190°C for 2-3 minutes.

HOMEMADE TACO SAUCE

With only 5 minutes preparation time, there would be no reason not to make your own sauce rather than use store bought. The combination of spices gives this sauce an authentic flavour that you won't find in a jar. The sauce freezes well so you could make extra to ensure you always have some to hand.

Preparation Time: **Total Time:** Makes 2 cups
10 minutes 10 minutes

INGREDIENTS

2 cups tomato puree
1 tbsp cumin powder
1 tbsp hot or smoked paprika
½ tsp onion powder
1 tsp garlic powder
1 tsp dried oregano
⅛ tsp coarse salt

⅛ tsp freshly ground black pepper
⅓ cup water
1 tsp white wine vinegar
1 tsp maple syrup
¼ to 1 tsp dried chili flakes
¼ to 1 tsp cayenne pepper

DIRECTIONS

Place all ingredients into a small saucepan and bring to a boil over medium heat. Reduce to low and simmer for 10 minutes in order for the sauce to thicken. If you prefer a thicker sauce leave it to simmer for 15 minutes

Remove from heat and allow to cool to room temperature.

The sauce will keep for up to 5 days in an airtight container in the fridge.

VEGAN SOUR CREAM

This quick and easy vegan sour cream is as close to the real thing as you can get! It is wonderfully rich and creamy, with a lovely flavour and perfect amount of 'tang'. Use it as a non-dairy alternative for dips and toppings.

Preparation Time: **Total Time:** Makes approx. 1 cup
15 minutes (+ overnight for 50 minutes
cashew nuts to soak)

INGREDIENTS

1 cup raw unsalted cashew nuts
(soaked overnight in water)
1 tbsp apple cider vinegar
Juice of 1 lemon

¼ tsp coarse salt
½ tsp nutritional yeast
⅓ - ½ cup water

DIRECTIONS

Drain cashews and place in a blender with vinegar, lemon, salt and start with ⅓ cup of water. Blend until very smooth, adding more water as required, depending on how thick you would like the sour cream.

Store in an airtight container in the fridge for up to 1 week.

CHIMICHURRI SAUCE

This popular piquant South American sauce differs according to which region it hails from. The Mexican version features a punchy flavorsome combination of herbs, garlic and lemon, amongst many other mouthwatering ingredients. It goes perfectly with almost anything- try it with tofu, drizzled over vegetables or even as a dipping sauce.

Preparation Time: **Total Time:**   Makes 1 ½ - 2 cups
5 minutes   5 minutes

INGREDIENTS

1 cup of good quality olive or vegetable oil

¼ cup lemon juice, freshly squeezed

½ cup fresh flat-leaf parsley, finely chopped

¼ cup fresh coriander leaves, finely chopped

2 tbsp garlic, finely chopped

1 tbsp red onion, finely chopped

1 tbsp dry oregano

1 tbsp dried chili flakes

1 tsp coarse salt (or more to taste)

½ tsp freshly ground black pepper

DIRECTIONS

Combine all ingredients in a large mixing bowl. Cover with cling film and allow to chill in the fridge for a minimum of 2 hours before serving for the flavours to marry.

Keep in an airtight container in the fridge for up to 2 weeks.

RESTAURANT STYLE SALSA

This tried and tested recipe for salsa is made in a food processor with tomatoes, coriander, and jalapenos. The perfect combination of ingredients provides a fresh, tangy and chunky salsa that's sure to be a real crowd pleaser.

Preparation Time: **Total Time:**   Makes approx. 4 cups
5 minutes   10 minutes

INGREDIENTS

2 (420g) cans chopped tomatoes, drained if you prefer a thicker salsa
3 cloves garlic, peeled
2 small fresh green chiles
1 bunch (about 2 cups loosely packed) fresh coriander
½ large white onion, finely chopped
1 tsp ground cumin

1 jalapeno, stem removed (and seeded, if you want less heat)
1 tsp coarse salt
1 tsp sugar
2 tbsp freshly squeezed lemon or lime juice
2 sprigs fresh oregano or 1 tsp dried oregano
¼ tsp freshly ground black pepper

DIRECTIONS

Place all ingredients in a food processor and pulse until you have reached your desired consistency. Taste to check if more salt or pepper is needed.

Chill, covered, for a minimum of 30 minutes for the flavours to marry.

Salas will keep for 3-4 days in an airtight container in the fridge.

SALSA VERDE

Salsa Verde is traditionally made with parsley, but this version features coriander, jalapenos and lime juice for a punchy Mexican alternative.

Preparation Time: **Total Time:**   Makes around 2 cups
5 minutes   10 minutes

INGREDIENTS

1 tbsp olive oil
650g tomatillos, husks removed, roughly chopped
1 large jalapeno pepper (seeds removed to reduce spice)
¼ medium onion

2 garlic cloves
½ cup coriander
1 tbsp lime juice
1 ½ tsp red wine vinegar
1 tsp dried oregano
½ tbsp coarse salt

DIRECTIONS

Heat olive oil in a large pan over medium-high heat. Add tomatillos, onions and jalapeno and saute for 3-4 minutes until slightly caramelised.

Remove from heat and carefully transfer into a blender. Add garlic, coriander, lime juice, red wine vinegar, oregano and salt and pulse until combined.

Transfer to an airtight container and refrigerate for 6 7 days.

VEGAN MEXICAN CHEESE

Here you have the only vegan cheese recipe you'll ever need to satisfy any cravings. Whether you want to sprinkle some cheese flavouring onto a fajita or burrito, spread some onto bread or use a Queso to pour over nachos, this simple easy and delicious cheese can seriously rival any dairy based version.

Preparation Time: **Total Time:** Makes 1-2 cups
10 mins 10 mins

INGREDIENTS

SHAKEABLE CHEESE:

1 cup unsalted raw cashews
3 ¼ tbsp nutritional yeast
¾ tsp coarse salt
¼ tsp freshly ground black pepper
½ tsp cumin
¼ tsp cayenne powder
½ tsp garlic powder
¼ tsp onion powder
¼ tsp paprika

SPREADABLE CHEESE:

1 ½ cups unsalted raw cashews
3 tbsp nutritional yeast
½ tsp coarse salt
¼ tsp garlic powder
½ tsp cumin
¼ tsp cayenne pepper
1-2 tbsp olive oil

QUESO:

1 cup of the spreadable cheese + hot water

DIRECTIONS

For the Shakeable Cheese:

Add all ingredients to a food processor a pulse in short bursts until a fine powder forms. You do not want to pulse for long periods at a time to prevent a puree from forming. Store in an airtight container in the fridge for up to 6 days and use to sprinkle on burritos, fajitas, tacos etc.

For the Spreadable Cheese:

Place the cashew nuts in a food processor and pulse until completely broken down until a smooth paste is formed. Scrape down the sides as you go along to ensure all of the nuts are incorporated. Add the cumin, garlic powder, cayenne, nutritional yeast and seasoning. Pulse until fully combined. Add olive oil, one tablespoon at a time and blend for 1-2 minutes to form a spread. Adding a second spoon of oil will produce a much thinner spread.

Store in an airtight container in the fridge for up to 6 days.

For the Queso:

Make the spreadable cheese and place desired portion into a medium bowl. Very slowly add hot water and continue to whisk after each addition to make a pourable cheese.

This cheese is perfect as a dip or to pour on top of nachos.

Store in an airtight container in the fridge for up to 6 days.

DESSERT

HORCHATA
(SWEET MEXICAN RICE MILK)

This cinnamon-vanilla frothy drink is a Mexican favorite, consisting of a milky, creamy yet dairy-free drink that has been thickened using rice milk. Perfect as a refreshing drink in the summer or heated up for a comforting warming drink when it's cold.

Preparation Time:
5 minutes (+ overnight for the rice to soak and 2-3 hours for Horchata to chill)

Total Time:
10 minutes

Makes 4 cups

INGREDIENTS

1 cup basmati rice
4 cups water
1 cinnamon stick

1 tbsp maple syrup
1 tsp cinnamon powder
½ tsp vanilla extract

DIRECTIONS

Place the rice and cinnamon stick in a glass bowl or large glass container and leave to soak overnight.

The following day, pour the entire contents - rice, water and cinnamon stick into a blender and add the vanilla and maple syrup. Blend until everything is pulsed and there are no large pieces left.

Pour the mixture through a sieve with a bowl underneath and discard the rice/cinnamon pieces.

Cover the bowl with cling film and chill in the fridge for 2-3 hours.

Serve in a glass over ice and add a pinch of cinnamon.

MEXICAN HOT CHOCOLATE

This wonderfully rich and creamy hot chocolate is spiced up with a pinch of cayenne pepper, and, of course, is 100% vegan. The flavour is also enhanced with cinnamon and nutmeg, making this the perfect warming drink for a cold winter's night. You could also spike it by adding a glug of Tequila!

Preparation Time: 5 minutes

Total Time: 10 mins

Makes 2 servings

INGREDIENTS

2 cups almond, coconut or soy milk

3 ½ tbsp cocoa powder

2-3 tbsp maple syrup

½ tsp ground cinnamon

¼ tsp nutmeg

¼ - ⅛ tsp cayenne

1 tsp vanilla extract

⅛ tsp coarse salt

DIRECTIONS

Pour milk into a small saucepan and bring to a gentle simmer over low heat.

Add cocoa powder, cinnamon, nutmeg, cayenne, vanilla, maple syrup, and salt and whisk constantly for a minute until all ingredients are fully combined.

Pour into heatproof glasses or mugs and serve immediately with an extra sprinkle of cinnamon on top of each mug.

CRISPY MEXICAN CHURROS

Churros are long, fluted cinnamon donuts that are crispy on the out-side and moist and fluffy on the inside. They are a truly decadent delight, which can be devoured plain or dipped in vegan chocolate sauce.

Preparation Time: **Total Time:** Makes 4 servings
5 minutes 15 minutes

INGREDIENTS

1 cup water
2 ½ tbsp white sugar
½ tsp coarse salt
2 tbsp vegetable oil
1 cup all-purpose flour

8-9 cups oil for frying
½ cup white sugar, for dusting
1 tsp ground cinnamon
Pastry bag, for piping

DIRECTIONS

Combine water, 2 ½ tablespoons sugar, salt and 2 tablespoons oil in a small saucepan and bring to a boil. Once boiling remove from heat.

Slowly stir in flour until mixture becomes a dough.

Heat the oil in a large pan over medium-high heat to 190°C.

Once hot place dough in a pastry bag and pipe strips into the hot dough Fry the dough in batches depending how big your pan is. You do not want to overcrowd the pan.

Fry churros for 3-5 minutes until golden and crisp. Once cooked, remove each churros using a slotted spoon and transfer to a paper towel lined plate.

Once all churros are cooked combine sugar and cinnamon in a sepa-rate bowl and sprinkle onto, ensuring all sides are well coated.

Serve immediately while hot and crispy.

CHILI CHOCOLATE AVOCADO MOUSSE

This chocolate avocado mousse is creamy and decadent, with a hint of chili to add a real Mexican kick. You'll be surprised to know this dessert is actually healthy as it is full of antioxidants and nutrients from the cacao powder and avocado - and best of all it takes just 5 minutes to prepare.

Preparation Time: 5 minutes

Total Time: 10 minutes (+ 3 hours for mousse to set in the fridge)

Makes 4-6 servings

INGREDIENTS

2 ripe avocados
½ cup raw cacao powder
½ cup full-fat coconut milk
¼ cup maple syrup (or more if you prefer it sweeter)

2 tsp vanilla extract
⅛ tsp coarse salt
⅛ - ¼ small red chili (depending on heat preference)
1 ½ tsp cinnamon, divided

DIRECTIONS

Place all ingredients, except ½ tsp cinnamon, into a food processor and blend until completely smooth.

Taste to check if you wish to add more maple syrup or chili.

Spoon mousse into serving bowls and dust each bowl with a pinch of cinnamon.

Cover with cling film and leave to set in the fridge for a minimum of 3 hours.

BUÑUELOS (CINNAMON-SUGAR CRISPS)

These light, crispy and sweet strips are sprinkled with cinnamon sugar and make a wonderful after dinner treat. They keep well in an airtight container and are great to have on hand to satisfy a sweet tooth.

Preparation Time: 5 minutes

Total Time: 30 minutes

Makes approx. 50 to 60 strips

INGREDIENTS

1 cup white granulated sugar
1 ½ tsp ground cinnamon
¼ tsp ground nutmeg

1 tsp vanilla powder (optional)
12 eight-inch plain tortillas
vegetable oil (for frying)

DIRECTIONS

In a large freezer bag or a deep, shallow dish combine sugar, cinnamon and nutmeg. Set aside.

Cut the tortillas into strips of around 3x2 inches.

Heat 1 inch of oil in a heavy bottomed pan. Heat the oil until it reaches 190°C. If you do not have a thermometer, test the oil with a piece of tortilla, which should sizzle when it touches the oil and should brown in about 2 to 3 minutes

Fry the tortillas in batches, making sure to not crowd the pan as this will prevent the Buñuelos from getting crispy. Once golden brown and crisp, remove the strips with a slotted spoon and transfer to a paper towel lined plate for a few seconds to remove some excess oil.

While hot place in the sugar-cinnamon mixture, making sure to mix well and fully coat.

The Buñuelos will keep for 3-4 days in an airtight container at room temperature.

MORE GREAT

HIGH CEDAR PRESS

TITLES

CPSIA information can be obtained
at www.ICGtesting.com
Printed in the USA
LVOW04s0452201216
517962LV00016B/891/P